Paul Revere

American Patriot

Colonial Leaders

Lord Baltimore *English Politician and Colonist*

Benjamin Banneker *American Mathematician and Astronomer*

William Bradford *Governor of Plymouth Colony*

Benjamin Franklin *American Statesman, Scientist, and Writer*

Anne Hutchinson *Religious Leader*

Cotton Mather *Author, Clergyman, and Scholar*

William Penn *Founder of Democracy*

John Smith *English Explorer and Colonist*

Miles Standish *Plymouth Colony Leader*

Peter Stuyvesant *Dutch Military Leader*

Revolutionary War Leaders

Benedict Arnold *Traitor to the Cause*

Nathan Hale *Revolutionary Hero*

Alexander Hamilton *First U.S. Secretary of the Treasury*

Patrick Henry *American Statesman and Speaker*

Thomas Jefferson *Author of the Declaration of Independence*

John Paul Jones *Father of the U.S. Navy*

Thomas Paine *Political Writer*

Paul Revere *American Patriot*

Betsy Ross *American Patriot*

George Washington *First U.S. President*

Paul
Revere

American Patriot

JoAnn A. Grote

Arthur M. Schlesinger, jr.
Senior Consulting Editor

...se Publishers

Philadelphia

Dedication: For my niece, Ashley Falvey

Produced by 21st Century Publishing and Communications, Inc.
New York, NY. http://www.21cpc.com

CHELSEA HOUSE PUBLISHERS
Editor in Chief Stephen Reginald
Production Manager Pamela Loos
Director of Photography Judy L. Hasday
Art Director Sara Davis
Managing Editor James D. Gallagher

Staff for *PAUL REVERE*
Project Editor/Publishing Coordinator Jim McAvoy
Associate Art Director Takeshi Takahashi
Series Design Keith Trego

The Chelsea House World Wide Web address is
http://www.chelseahouse.com

3 5 7 9 8 6 4 2

Library of Congress Cataloging-in-Publication Data

Grote, JoAnn A.
Paul Revere / by JoAnn A. Grote.
80 pp. cm. — (Revolutionary War Leaders series)
Includes bibliographical references and index.
Summary: A biography of the silversmith and Revolutionary War hero who made the famous ride to warn American troops of the British approach to Lexington and Concord.
ISBN 0-7910-5355-5 (hc)   ISBN 0-7910-5698-8 (pb)
1. Revere, Paul, 1735–1818—Juvenile literature. 2. Statesmen—Massachusetts—Biography—Juvenile literature. 3. Massachusetts—Biography—Juvenile literature. 4. Massachusetts—History—Revolution, 1775–1783—Juvenile literature. [1. Revere, Paul, 1735–1818. 2. United States—History—Revolution, 1775–1783—Biography. 3. Silversmiths.] I. Title. II. Series.
F69.R43G76   1999
974.4'03'092—dc21   99-27369
[B]   CIP

Publisher's Note: In Colonial and Revolutionary War America, there were no standard rules for spelling, punctuation, capitalization, or grammar. Some of the quotations that appear in the Colonial Leaders and Revolutionary War Leaders series come from original documents and letters written during this time in history. Original quotations reflect writing inconsistencies of the period.

Contents

A bustling Boston in the time of Paul Revere. The Old State House, center, stands on an active King Street that today is called State Street.

1

When Is Paul's Birthday?

Do you know what day you were born? No one knows exactly what day Paul Revere was born. We do know he has two birth dates. When Paul was born, people used the Old Style Calendar. Soon after that they started using the calendar we use today. By these two calendar systems, Paul's two birth dates were 10 days apart.

Paul was **baptized** on January 1, 1735, by our calendar. Babies in Christian families were baptized as soon as possible after they were born. So Paul was probably born close to January 1. Maybe he was born on that day.

Paul was born at home, like all babies in the 1700s. He was carried to church through cold winter weather to be baptized. It was a chilly trip for a new baby. Churches weren't heated, so even inside Paul must have been very cold.

He wasn't the only Paul in the family. His father's name was Paul, too. His mother and sister were both named Deborah. Actually, Paul's father had another name—Apollos Rivoire. It was a French name, because he was born in France. When Apollos was a teenager, his parents sent him to America to seek a better life. Apollos settled in Boston and learned the skills necessary to become a silversmith. He soon opened his own shop and got married. Apollos Rivoire changed his name to Paul Revere, so that it would be easier for his customers to say. Mr. Revere also gave this name to his first son.

Young Paul was born in the town of Boston, in Massachusetts. Boston wasn't part of the United States back then. The United States didn't exist yet. No one knew that one day Paul would help start the country we now call the United States.

At that time, Boston belonged to Britain. So did Massachusetts. Massachusetts wasn't a state at that time. It was called a colony. It was ruled by the British king.

Paul lived in a busy house. By the time he was nine, Paul and his sister Deborah had seven younger brothers and sisters. As the oldest boy, Paul probably spent lots of time caring for, and playing with, his younger brothers and sisters.

All year round Paul's house smelled of wood smoke from the large kitchen fireplace. Mrs. Revere made all the meals over the fireplace. Paul probably had the same chores as most boys in Boston: carrying wood for the fireplace, cleaning the ashes out of the fireplace and taking them outside, and carrying pails of water home from the town well.

Most homes didn't have large living rooms and bedrooms. The fireplace made the kitchen

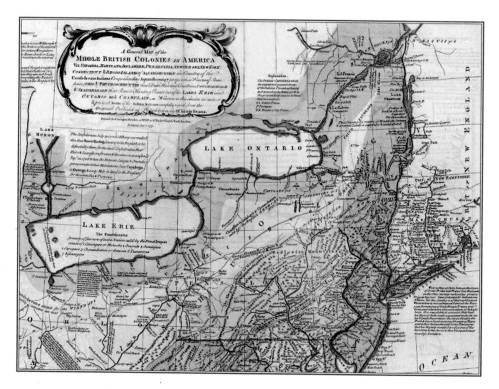

A map of the British colonies in America. For 100 years before the Revolutionary War, the British had been fighting with the French about control over colonial territories in America and Canada.

the warmest room in the house during winter. Paul and his brothers and sisters, like most people, spent a good deal of time there.

Paul had brown hair, brown eyes, and a round face. He dressed like all the other boys in Boston. He wore shirts with big sleeves. His pants stopped just below his knees. Boys wore knee buckles to keep their pant legs tight. The buckles helped keep their knee-high stockings up, too. The stockings sometimes slipped down when they ran, even with knee buckles.

When Paul wasn't doing chores in the house, or playing with his brothers and sisters, or going to church, he spent time in his father's shop. The shop might have been a room in their house. Or it might have been a small building close to the house.

Mr. Revere was a goldsmith and silversmith. He made all kinds of things out of gold and silver: teapots, trays, sugar bowls, pitchers, buckles for shoes, jewelry, and thimbles. First he melted the silver in a brick furnace. It was very hot. He wore a leather apron to protect his clothes. Paul had to be careful so he didn't get burned.

Paul liked to watch his father work, to see the melted silver become something beautiful. Paul knew that one day he too wanted to make beautiful things from silver.

Besides playing or doing chores or watching his father work, Paul had to learn to read. Massachusetts made the first law in America saying parents must teach their children to read. It didn't say children must go to school. It didn't say they must learn to write or to do arithmetic.

Paul learned to read. He also learned to write and do arithmetic. There were two kinds of schools in Massachusetts: writing schools were for children who would be tradesmen and shopkeepers, and Latin schools were for children who planned to go to college some day.

It is believed Paul studied at North Writing School. North Writing was on Love Lane. It was a two-story, wooden building. Reading was taught on one floor of the school. Writing was taught on another floor. There weren't any girls in Paul's classes. Only boys went to North Writing. There was no summer vacation either. Classes were held all year long.

If Paul went to school, he probably learned to read from the *New England Primer.* It was the first schoolbook in Boston. Many things in the *New England Primer* were taught in rhymes.

If Paul learned reading at home, he might have learned from a hornbook. A hornbook wasn't really a book at all. It was made of wood and shaped like a paddle. It was very small— only five inches high and two inches wide. On one side was paper.

The *New England Primer* was printed in Boston in 1690. It was not only the first schoolbook in Boston, but also the only school textbook in all of the New England colonies for 50 years. The *New England Primer* was used by schools for almost 150 years.

The paper was covered by a horn. That's why it was called a hornbook. The horns came from animals. People heated the horns until they could lay flat. The heat also made the horn clear, so people could see through it. The horn kept the paper from getting wet or torn.

The alphabet in lowercase letters was listed on the first two lines of the paper. The alphabet in capital letters made up the next two lines. On the bottom half of the paper was a prayer.

Children would read the paper out loud. They read it over and over and over. After reading it out loud many times they would know their ABCs. They would know how to read some words, too.

Paul had lots of fun places to play in Boston. At Boston's ponds he could float wooden boats and rafts. He could catch toads and frogs. One of the ponds was called Frog Pond. In winter, he could skate on the ponds.

A Boston law said children couldn't swim in the ocean. Boys swam in the ocean anyway. When Paul was a man he drew a picture with boys jumping off a large Boston dock into the harbor to swim. Maybe he drew it because he liked to swim so much when he was a boy.

The streets Paul walked and ran on had funny names: Frog Lane, Beer Lane, Fish Street, Love Lane, Turnagain Alley. What would he have seen in the streets? Pigs and chickens sometimes roamed the streets. Women going to market carried baskets on their arms. Men selling things pulled wooden carts. "Get your oysters!" or "Fresh pumpkins!" the men would sing out. Paul might have to stop to yank up his stockings.

By the shipyards he heard the sound of hammers. People were always busy building and fixing ships there. Paul saw many different ships every day.

Boston was on a **peninsula**. Only one skinny piece of land connected Boston to the shore. That piece of land was called The Neck. Boston was built in a harbor on the Atlantic Ocean.

Many huge wooden docks, called **wharves**, lined the harbor. Some were built so far out in the harbor that ships tied up to them.

The largest wharves were so long and so wide that buildings were built on one side of them. Paul's family lived on a wharf when he was seven. The smell of salt water and fish was always around.

Paul's childhood was spent among the wharves of Boston. In the busy harbor he saw ships from all over the world bringing goods to the people of the colonies.

When he went to bed at night he heard waves lapping against the wharf. When he woke up in the morning he still heard the waves. He heard seagulls calling too. Men also called to each other as they unloaded ships. The wheels of wooden carts thumped over the wharf's planks.

The wharf was Paul's front yard. Each day was a new adventure. What ships would he see? Ships brought people from all over the world. Every day he'd hear many different languages.

It was a fun place to play hide-and-seek. Wooden barrels and trunks and crates were unloaded and piled along the wharf. Inside them were molasses, tea, sugar, raisins, rice, and cloth. There were a lot of things people in Boston wanted but couldn't make or grow themselves. These thing came by ship. Boston was a big, busy harbor.

Paul's family moved to Fish Street when he was eight. His home was still near a wharf, but not on one anymore. If Paul wanted to see far out into the harbor, he would have climbed Beacon Hill. The highest place in Boston, other than Beacon Hill, was the steeple of the Old North Church. Paul wanted to climb that, too. One day, he found a way.

Paul Revere, pictured with his silversmith's tools and a teapot. Paul became a skilled silversmith and took over the family business after his father died. Some of the beautiful things Paul made may still be seen in museums today.

2

Paul Grows Up

When Paul was a teenager, he and six friends became bell ringers for Old North Church. One day a week he rang the bells for two hours.

Paul had to climb narrow, winding stairs almost 10 stories high to get to the top of the steeple. From there Paul could see the mainland across the Charles River.

Ringing the bells wasn't easy. There were eight bells of different sizes. Some weighed hundreds of pounds. Each different-sized bell had its own very special sound.

Paul's job was very important. Most people didn't have watches or clocks. There were no televisions or radios or sirens. The ringing of the church bells told people when something was happening.

The bells rang many times each week. They rang for people coming to church on Sundays. They rang when someone died, announcing the funerals. They rang when there was a fire in town, calling for help. And they rang to start the town markets in the morning. No one could do business at the markets before the bells rang.

Paul liked church bells. After the Revolutionary War, Paul and his son, Joseph Warren Revere, ran a company that made almost 400 church bells. Some still hang in old New England church steeples to this very day.

Sometimes the way the bells were rung gave people even more information. The number of times a bell rang when someone died told the person's age. They even signaled whether the person was a man or a woman.

Paul not only rang church bells, he also

began to learn from his father. Mr. Revere was teaching Paul to be a silversmith.

Most boys were done with school when they became teenagers. Then it was time for them to learn a trade or a job. They had to learn to support themselves. Most boys learned their jobs as **apprentices**.

Each apprentice worked with an adult called a master. Each master taught the apprentice certain skills. Sometimes the master had to give the apprentice clothes, food, and a place to sleep. Other apprentices lived at home. They only went to the job during the day.

Boys worked as apprentices for four to seven years. They had to be 21 before they could own their own shop. This way people would know the boys had learned their trade well.

It's a good thing Paul learned the silversmith trade as well as he did. When he was 19, his father died. Paul wrote later that his father "left a good name and seven children."

Now Paul was the oldest man in his family.

He had to help his mother care for his younger brothers and sisters. Paul had to make enough money to pay the rent and buy food and clothes for everyone.

He couldn't own his father's shop because he wasn't 21 yet. So his mother was officially the shop owner, but it was Paul who worked to make the money for the family. He made the silver pieces. Paul was no longer an apprentice. Now he was a master, and his 15-year-old brother, Tom, was his apprentice.

Instead of Mr. Revere, now Paul was the one melting silver in a hot furnace, and being very careful not to spill it. Paul was the one who hammered out pieces of silver. He was the one who made wax molds for pretty teapot handles. He put his name or initials on the bottom of pitchers and sugar bowls. That way people would always know who made them—even though no one knew yet that one day Paul would be a hero.

Paul made knee buckles, punch bowls, rings,

buttons, baby rattles, dog collars, and tiny picture frames. He even made a silver chain for a man's pet squirrel. He became one of the best silversmiths in the colonies.

He wrote down how much money his customers owed him in books called ledgers. In his first ledger he wrote, "This is my book for me to . . ." He never finished the sentence.

Paul wrote a list in his ledger of some things he gave Tom: knee buckles, a silk handkerchief, stockings, and a wig.

Two years later a war started between Britain and France. Both countries wanted America for themselves. They had been fighting over land in America for over 100 years. They would fight a war for a few years. Then they would be at peace for a few years.

This war was called the French and Indian War. It was also called the Seven Years' War because it lasted for seven years. By this time, some groups of American Indians had become friends with the French and helped them to fight the British; some other groups of Indians had become friends with the British and helped them to fight the French.

Paul knew all about the wars. Because Boston was under the rule of the British, it fought against the French during the war. The people of Boston had always made sure the city could defend itself if it was attacked. It helped that Boston was built on a peninsula. Enemies could only get to the city by land through the skinny Neck.

The citizens of Boston worried most about being attacked by enemy ships. They built a fort called the Castle. It was on an island in the harbor, between Boston and the ocean. If enemy ships came into the harbor, Bostonians would hear the cannons from the fort. They could then get ready for the enemy if the Castle's cannons didn't sink the ships first.

There were two **batteries** in Boston that held cannons and **ammunition**. One was on the north end of town and one on the south end of town.

Thousands of young men from Boston had fought against the French. Now it was Paul's turn. He was made an officer. The army gave him many things to carry: a lamp, a kettle, a bowl, a plate, two spoons, a powder horn, a bullet pouch, a blanket, a knapsack, and a wooden bottle.

Along with many other young soldiers, Paul started his long walk north to Fort William Henry on Lake George. This was in what is now part of New York State. Paul fully expected to fight the French, but he didn't. He never saw any French soldiers. The French soldiers were off fighting battles in other parts of New England.

It was still scary at the fort, however. Many of the soldiers became very sick and died there. There were also a lot of soldiers killed by different Native Americans.

In November 1756 Paul and the other Massachusetts soldiers were sent home. Paul returned to his silversmith shop, glad to be alive and safe.

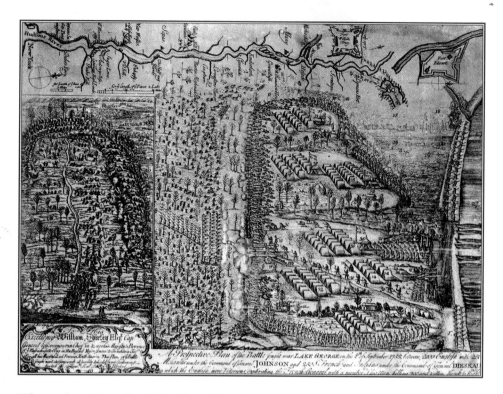

The plan for the Battle of Lake George, New York. Although Paul marched with the Massachusetts army to Fort William Henry on Lake George, he never saw action there and returned to Boston.

The next summer, in 1757, Paul married Sara Orne. He called her Sary. Sary and Paul's first child was born the following spring. They named her Deborah, after Paul's mother. Paul called his little baby girl Debby.

The house was filled with people, just the

way Paul liked it. There were Paul's mother, Paul, Sary, Debby, and Paul's brothers and sisters. Sometimes Paul's other apprentices lived with them too. Paul's brothers and sisters, as well as his children, would one day grow up and leave Paul's home. But Paul's mother lived with him for the rest of her life.

The Reveres had a dog, too. It was a small dog. Boston had a law at that time that said people could only have dogs that were under a foot high. Paul also bought a horse.

It takes lots of money to care for so many people. So Paul began doing other things besides working with silver and gold. He liked to do a lot of different things. He made engravings, which were used to make pictures. He published a **hymnbook**. He helped Boston get its first streetlights.

Paul also became a dentist. He whittled false teeth from hippopotamus tusks and teeth. His newspaper ad said his false teeth looked "as well as Natural."

Sary and Paul had eight children. Two died very young. They named their only boy Paul, just like his dad. Paul Revere loved all of his children very much.

One of his children caught a disease called smallpox. Smallpox looks like chicken pox, but smallpox can kill people. The town leaders ordered Paul to take his child to the **pesthouse**. Paul said no. Pesthouses were places where sick people stayed so other people wouldn't catch their sickness. People were often afraid to go to the pesthouses because they would usually get worse there.

So the town leaders made Paul and his family stay at home until everyone in the family was well again. A flag was placed outside the house to let people know there was somebody with smallpox inside. A guard stood outside the door to see that no one left or entered the house for more than a month.

Paul and Sary's last child was born in the spring of 1773. Soon after, Sary got sick and died.

Four months later, sadly, their newborn baby girl died, too.

It was hard for Paul and his mother to care for the six children. So in October, Paul got married again. His second wife's name was Rachel Walker.

Two months after Paul and Rachel were married, something happened that changed Paul's life forever. And mine. And yours.

It was the Boston Tea Party. The Boston Tea Party would lead to another war. This time, Paul wouldn't be fighting the French. He'd be fighting the British. And the war would make him a hero.

Stamp tax collectors were sometimes hoisted up "liberty poles" by angry colonists. Bostonians were the first to protest the Stamp Act, but before very long other colonists did the same. The British were soon forced to stop the act.

3

A Tea Party

Britain's war against the French cost a lot of money. Because the war was being fought over who should control America, the British thought that the Americans should pay some of the costs. So Britain began putting taxes on things the colonists needed. The British intended to use the money collected to help them pay for the war.

First Britain passed a new law called the Stamp Act. This law said the colonists must pay a tax on all business papers—newspapers, wills, certificates, and legal documents. The colonists did not like to be taxed, and they got mad. People protested against the Stamp Act. Protesters sometimes tied stamp tax collectors to liberty poles or liberty trees. And sometimes the protesters even covered the stamp tax collectors with sticky tar and feathers, and then chased them out of town.

So the British ended the Stamp Act and stopped collecting the stamp taxes. But they soon started taxing other things. Again the colonists fought the taxes. Finally Britain ended the taxes on everything except tea.

The colonists were still very angry. They liked tea and drank a lot of it each year. With the tax, tea became very expensive. To protest the tax they agreed that they would not buy any more tea from Britain. Like many other Bostonians, Paul and Rachel stopped buying tea, too. "Children, this is the last cup of tea you will get for a long time," Rachel said to her family as she poured her last pot of tea.

British law said all its people would have a lawmaker who represented them. The British laws were also the laws of colonies. But none of the lawmakers in Britain were colonists and the lawmakers in Britain were not chosen by the colonists. Many colonists didn't think Britain had the right to tax them. "No taxation without representation!" they cried.

Not everyone thought Britain was wrong. People who thought Britain was right were called **Loyalists**, because they were loyal to the British king. People who thought Britain was wrong were called **Patriots**. Paul was a Patriot.

Patriots feared that if Britain were allowed to take away one of the colonists' rights it would surely take away more. Paul wanted to do something about the problem. He became a leader of the **Sons of Liberty**.

The Sons of Liberty was a secret club. The Sons had a secret language and wore special medals around their necks to know who belonged. There were Sons of Liberty in all the largest towns and many small ones.

Paul and the other leaders had their own club

British soldiers fire on Bostonians. Paul was so disturbed by the shooting of ordinary people that he engraved, printed, and sold copies of a picture of his interpretation of the event that he called the "Boston Massacre." He hoped his picture would motivate the citizens of Boston and the other colonists to fight the British.

called the **Long Room Club.** It was more secret than the Sons of Liberty. One of Paul's best friends, Dr. Joseph Warren, was also a member.

There were many soldiers in Boston and the citizens didn't like it. Tensions mounted. In March 1770 a small argument turned bloody when shots were fired by a British soldier. The event, which came to be known as the Boston Massacre, sparked more conflict between the colonists and Britain.

In November 1773 three British ships filled with tea landed in Boston Harbor. Paul and the Sons of Liberty were angry. They didn't want the ships to unload the tea.

There were great tensions between the Bostonians and the many British soldiers stationed there. On March 5, 1770, a boy had a small fight with a British soldier. The boy called for help and the church bells began to ring. More than 400 townspeople rushed out of their homes and shops.

Angry people threw chunks of ice at the soldiers. Suddenly, a gun was fired, then, another, and another. When the shooting stopped, five people were dead and another six were wounded. Paul was very upset and drew a picture of the incident. He called the event the Boston Massacre.

Dr. Joseph Warren, an important colonial leader and a friend of Paul's, became the head of the Massachusetts militia and later was killed in the Battle of Bunker Hill.

The governor was a Loyalist. He ordered the tea unloaded and told the British soldiers to fire cannons at the ships if they tried to leave.

On November 30, 1773, Paul Revere went on the first of his many rides as an **express rider**.

He and five other riders rode to towns along the coast. They told the Sons of Liberty in those towns what was happening in Boston. The Patriots promised not to let any tea be unloaded in their towns either.

So what was going to happen to the tea?

The Sons of Liberty came up with a plan. On December 16, 1773, Paul Revere and some other Sons darkened their faces using paint, grease, and black soot from lamps. They covered their hair and slipped blankets over their shoulders.

They didn't want people to know who they were. Paul and his friends hoped people would think they looked like Indians.

Paul knew what he was doing was very dangerous. He might be caught and thrown in jail. He might lose his house and business and horse and money. But he believed what he was doing was right. He picked up his axe, like the other Sons, and was on his way.

His heart must have pounded fast as he slipped through the dark, crooked, narrow streets to the wharves. There the three ships were anchored. He watched out for British soldiers. He didn't see any.

He was surprised to see townspeople crowding the wharf. The Sons of Liberty's secret plan had leaked out. If all those people knew the secret, surely the British soldiers must know, too. What if the soldiers tried to stop them?

Paul kept going. What he was doing was too important to stop. The other Sons kept going, too. People might know their secret, but they didn't know who they were. As long as they weren't recognized, and the soldiers didn't attack them, they would be all right.

Paul and the other Sons climbed on board the three ships. The townspeople watched silently. Paul opened a wooden tea box with his axe. He dumped the tea and the box into the water.

The harbor was brown with tea when they were done. In three hours 10,000 pounds of tea had been cast into the water!

It was almost dawn when Paul and the Sons

Angry colonists in Boston disguised themselves as Indians and dumped 10,000 pounds of British tea into Boston Harbor. This was known as the Boston Tea Party.

left the ships. They had not touched anything else aboard the ships. They had not hurt anyone, and no one had hurt them. Paul could hardly believe the soldiers hadn't tried to stop them.

As they left the scene, the townspeople marched up the wharf with them. One of the group played a tune on a **fife**. When they reached the head of the wharf, a window suddenly flew open. The British **admiral** stuck out his head. He'd watched the whole thing.

Paul and his friends had been saved by the townspeople who knew their secret. The admiral knew he did not have enough soldiers to fight thousands of townspeople. He would not fire cannons at the tea throwers with so many townspeople around.

"You have got to pay the fiddler yet," he told Paul and the others below his window.

> After the bold and daring Boston Tea Party, people in Boston began singing a song. Part of it went like this:
>
> Rally Mohawks! bring
>   out your axes,
>
> And tell King George
>   we'll pay no taxes
>
> On his foreign tea . . .
>
> Our Warren's there and
>   bold Revere
>
> With hands to do, and
>   words to cheer
>
> For Liberty and laws . . .

Paul knew what that meant. Somehow they would have to pay for what they'd done.

The people in Boston wanted the people in other towns to know about the Boston Tea Party. Right away they wrote down what happened.

They needed someone they could trust to take the papers to the other towns.

So Paul climbed on his horse, took the papers, and dashed away. It was a long ride to New York and Philadelphia. It took him 11 days to make the trip.

Paul brought good news back with him. The Sons of Liberty in New York and Philadelphia thought the Boston Tea Party had been the right thing to do.

The people in Boston were still worried. The Sons of Liberty weren't the only people sending letters to friends. The admiral and governor sent news of the Boston Tea Party back to Britain. What would King George say about it? Would Boston have to "pay the fiddler," as the admiral had warned?

British troops land in Boston to close the port as punishment for the Boston Tea Party. The colonists were angry that no goods could be delivered by ship, so they had a second tea party. Paul Revere took this news to colonists in other cities and towns.

Spy!

4

It took a very long time for the ship to cross the ocean with the news for King George. It took an even longer time for the ship to come back with news from King George.

In May, five months after the Boston Tea Party took place, a ship from Britain brought news of the colonists' punishment. Beginning the first day of June, Boston would be closed to all boats and ships. It would stay closed until the people of Boston paid for the tea. The king also sent many ships carrying British troops to Boston to guard the port and enforce his punishment.

Now the only way anyone would be able to get into Boston or leave it would be by the Neck. Most of the people in Boston were used to getting all of the things they needed to live from ships. Now they would no longer be able to do so.

To protest the punishment from the king, Boston's Sons of Liberty held a second tea party.

Once more, Paul saddled up his horse. Again he took the news to other Patriots in New York and Philadelphia. More riders took the news to other towns.

Patriots everywhere were absolutely outraged at the punishment handed down by King George. The people from the towns and the countryside, from Massachusetts and the other colonies, told Paul they would help the people of Boston however they could.

On June 1 the bells in the Old North Church, which Paul had rung as a teenager, rang and rang and rang. They didn't ring with cheerful news, or news of a funeral, or to tell the people that the markets were open. They rang because the wharves were silent. The only ships in the harbor were British warships.

The people of Boston still didn't pay for the tea. People in other Massachusetts towns and the other colonies sent food to help feed the people of Boston. Of course, the food had to be brought into Boston by horse and wagon, using that skinny piece of land called the Neck, instead of more easily by ship as it usually was.

> The Old North Church, also called Christ's Church, still stands in Boston. The steeple was blown down in a hurricane in 1804. The church built a new steeple, and the same eight bells that Paul Revere rang as a teenager still hang there today.

King George sent things to Boston, too. He sent more soldiers and warships. Boston's streets were filled with the hated **redcoats**, as the British soldiers were called. The soldiers marched on the town **common** in their red outfits with black three-cornered hats and black boots, carrying their guns, called muskets.

The children of Patriots teased the soldiers. They called them **lobster-backs**, because of their red coats.

There were so many soldiers in Boston that people were forced to let the soldiers stay in their houses. Paul Revere had such a large family that there wasn't room for any soldiers at his house.

Many people worried that war would start very soon with all the British soldiers arriving in Boston. They packed up everything they could, took their families, and left.

Paul and his family didn't leave. Paul had new, important, secret duties. He was one of 30 spies for the Patriots. He said, "We . . . took turns, two by two, to watch the soldiers, by patrolling the streets all night." He couldn't watch the soldiers very well if he left Boston.

It was extremely important to know what the soldiers were planning. They had already surprised Charlestown, the town across the river. They had taken the town's ammunition.

King George III of Britain. After the Boston Tea Party, the king wanted to have some colonial leaders arrested and sent to Britain.

Paul didn't want what happened to Boston to happen to any other towns.

One night a spy heard the soldiers were planning to take the ammunition from Fort

British troops in Boston. Before war broke out, the city became so full of soldiers that citizens were forced to take the hated "redcoats" into their homes.

William and Mary. That fort belonged to colonists in New Hampshire.

It was not easy to get out of Boston now. People could not leave without a pass from the British general. Paul had to sneak out of town to get the news to other Patriots and he could not ride out over the Neck. He kept a small rowboat hidden beneath a wharf. A Patriot on the other side of the river loaned him a horse.

Fort William and Mary was 60 miles away. It was very hard for the horse to run on the snowy, icy road. Paul finally reached the fort. A man who saw Paul that day said that Paul's horse looked so bad that he was "nearly done" when they got there.

When the British arrived, they were very unhappy to find that the fort was empty. Before they arrived, the Patriots had moved their weapons and ammunition to safety.

The British soldiers were getting tired of this game. They knew someone had warned the Patriots. They thought it might be Paul, but they couldn't prove it. Paul was just too tricky for them to catch him. The soldiers began calling Paul "a storm warning."

Another time, Paul heard that the soldiers might try to take the ammunition from the town of Salem. Paul and some other spies rowed out into the harbor by the Castle. Paul hoped to find out if what he'd heard was true.

The British soldiers saw them. Paul and his friends were chased, caught, and arrested. They were prisoners at the Castle for two days and three nights.

While Paul was behind bars and unable to warn the other Patriots, the British soldiers surprised Salem and took their ammunition. When Paul and his friends got out of prison, they wrote a note of apology. They told the Patriots in Salem that they were sorry for not warning them about the British.

Back in Britain, King George was mad that the British soldiers hadn't frightened Boston into paying for the tea. He wanted his general to arrest the Patriot leaders and send them to Britain to be put on trial. The Sons of Liberty knew that if that happened, the Patriot leaders would surely be hung.

In April 1775 it looked like the soldiers were getting ready to attack again, but Paul wasn't sure where. Dr. Joseph Warren and Paul knew that two of the colonies' most important Patriot leaders, John Hancock and Samuel Adams, were staying in Lexington. It was important the leaders know that the British soldiers might soon be on the move.

Paul quickly snuck out of Boston. He rode first to Lexington to deliver the news. Then the Patriots in the town of Concord were warned. They put their bullets in sacks and hid the sacks in the swamps near town. Then they buried the town cannon in an out-of-the-way field.

Every day it was getting more and more difficult to sneak out of Boston. What if he didn't make it out next time to warn the others? Paul knew he had to come up with a better plan.

John Hancock was a Boston merchant and one of the richest men in America in his day. He had a mansion on Beacon Hill and a fleet of ships. One of the signers of the Declaration of Independence, he was later elected president of the Continental Congress. John Hancock had hoped to become commander of the American Army, but instead, that position went to George Washington. In 1780 Hancock became governor of Massachusetts.

On the way back home, Paul stopped in Charlestown. He had an idea and shared his plan with a friend. If the Patriots saw the soldiers leave Boston, he thought, they could hang lanterns in the steeple of the Old North Church as a signal. Two lanterns would mean the soldiers went by boats or ships. One lantern would mean that they went over the Neck, by land. Mr. Newman, who took care of the church, could easily hang the lanterns.

Without Samuel Adams, there might not have been an American Revolution. He created the first Committee of Correspondence, to keep each of the colonies informed about what the British were doing in the other colonies. He was also the chief organizer of the Boston Tea Party and one of the signers of the Declaration of Independence.

Two days later, a stable boy came running, out of breath, to Paul. He told Paul he'd heard British officers talking about how the soldiers would be marching to Concord the very next day.

Paul's friend, Dr. Joseph Warren, was in charge of the Patriots in Boston. "About 10 o'clock

Dr. Warren sent in great haste for me," Paul wrote later, "and begged that I would immediately set off for Lexington."

Paul and Warren were sure the soldiers intended to arrest John Hancock and Samuel Adams. Someone had to warn them, and Dr. Warren knew Paul was the right man for the job. Paul was to warn people along the way that the soldiers were coming. Other riders were sent by other routes in case Paul didn't make it.

Paul ran to Mr. Newman's house, but British soldiers were staying there. Paul looked through the window and saw the soldiers playing cards. How could he give Mr. Newman the message about the lanterns? What would he do now?

Paul Revere's famous ride, in which, at great risk, he warned people throughout the towns and countryside. Some later said that he did not shout, "The British are coming!" Instead, he may have been yelling, "The regulars are coming out!"

The Ride

Suddenly Mr. Newman stepped out of the shadows. Was Paul glad to see him!

Mr. Newman had told the soldiers he was going to bed. Then he crawled out a window and waited for Paul. Paul told him to hurry to the Old North Church and hang two lanterns.

Then Paul rushed home, grabbed what he needed, and started off. His little dog trotted along behind him. Paul stopped to pick up two friends. Together, they hurried to his hidden rowboat.

In his rush, Paul had forgotten his riding spurs. He dashed off a note, tucked the note into his dog's collar, and sent the dog home.

Paul had also forgotten some cloth to wrap around the oars to make them quieter when he was rowing the boat in the water.

The Patriots weren't the only ones to use the Old North Church. British General Gage watched the Battle of Bunker Hill from inside the steeple. Major Pitcairn, who led the British soldiers in the Battle of Lexington and the Battle of Bunker Hill, is buried in a tomb beneath the church.

One of his friends knew a woman who lived nearby and could be trusted. Paul's friend whistled from below her window. The woman looked out. He told her they needed some cloth. The woman took off her petticoat and tossed it out the window. Paul tore it in two and tied the pieces around the two oars.

Soon Paul's dog was back with his spurs. Paul and his friends climbed into the boat and pushed off from the shore.

Then came the scariest part. They had to row right past a British warship. Paul must have wished April 18, 1775, were a cloudy, foggy night. Fog would have hidden him from the soldiers on the warship. Instead, the night was bright with moonlight.

Paul could see British soldiers were crossing the river, too. They were on the other side of the warship. He thought there must be 1,000 of them.

Paul looked back at Boston. Two lanterns hung in the steeple. Newman had climbed the narrow stairs and done his job. Had Paul's friend in Charlestown seen the lanterns?

They rowed past the huge warship. His friends tried hard to keep the oars from splashing. Paul was glad he'd tied cloth on them to make them quieter. He looked up at the ship towering above them. Would the soldiers see them? Would they fire their guns at them?

The soldiers didn't do any of those things, because they didn't see Paul's little boat.

A friend of Paul was waiting for him on the other side. He'd seen the lantern. Paul told him about the soldie river. His friend would now wake Sons of Liberty in Charlestown.

John Hancock was elected president of the Continental Congress and was one of the signers of the Declaration of Independence. He also became governor of Massachusetts.

One of the richest men in town had his best horse waiting for Paul. The horse was named Brown Beauty, and it was one of the fastest horses in Massachusetts. Paul was happy with the horse. His friends warned him to be careful. British officers had been watching the roads that day.

Riding a magnificent horse, Paul started off toward Lexington by the shortest road. This is what he said happened next:

"The moon shone bright. . . . I saw two Officers on Horseback, standing under the shade of a Tree, in a narrow part of the road. I was near enough to see their Holsters. . . . One of them started his horse towards me."

The other officer went up the road to stop Paul if he tried to escape.

Paul didn't have time to think. He turned his horse around quickly. They galloped across muddy land toward another road.

The British officer's horse got stuck in the mud. Paul's horse didn't. Soon Paul was on the other road. He knew it would take longer to get to Lexington by this road. Would he get there in time to warn Hancock and Adams?

At the first town he came to he woke the

captain of the town's **minutemen**. Paul told him to wake up his men before the British soldiers came. Paul didn't have any time to waste. Next he headed toward Lexington.

Paul woke people in almost every farmhouse along the road. Farmers threw on their clothes, grabbed their guns, and headed down the road to join the minutemen.

Soon Paul heard church bells ringing. They were ringing to tell people the British soldiers were coming.

It was almost midnight when Paul reached Lexington. He hurried to the pastor's house. That's where Hancock and Adams were staying. Eight men were guarding the house. They told Paul everyone in the house had gone to bed. The people didn't want to be awakened.

Paul was in no mood to hear that after his long ride. "You'll have noise enough before long! The **Regulars** are out!" he hollered as he banged on the door.

John Hancock recognized his voice. "Come

Samuel Adams created the Committee of Correspondence to provide information to all the colonies. He was also a signer of the Declaration of Independence.

in, Revere," he called. "We're not afraid of you."

The guards let Paul inside. He quickly told John Hancock and Samuel Adams that the British soldiers were approaching.

John Hancock didn't want to leave. He ordered his sword and gun. He wanted to fight the British with the minutemen. Samuel Adams told Hancock that he was too important to the Patriots to risk dying.

How do we know what happened the night of Paul Revere's ride? Three times Paul Revere wrote down what happened that night. He told his children, grandchildren, and great-grandchildren what happened, too. His children told other people about the petticoat that covered the oars that famous night and about the dog who ran home with Paul's message and brought back his spurs.

Paul had risked his life to save these men. Instead of leaving, they argued. They kept arguing while Paul had something to eat.

They were still arguing when Paul and another spy left to warn Concord. Another Patriot and friend joined them on the road.

Paul and his friends ran into more trouble on their way to Concord. They were confronted by four British officers who were pointing their pistols at them. "Stop," said one of the British. "If you go an inch further, you are a dead man."

Paul and his friends tried to keep going anyway. The officers yelled that if they didn't get off the road and into the pasture beside it, the officers would shoot them.

Paul and his friends turned toward the pasture. One of his friends jumped his horse over a stone wall and got away. Paul saw a wooded area nearby. He thought if he could get to the woods, he could jump off his horse and run through the trees to get away.

But when he got to the woods, six more officers jumped out. They were all pointing their pistols at him! He was ordered to get off his horse. He did.

One of the British officers asked them where they came from, and what time they left. Paul answered truthfully.

"Sir, may I have your name?" the officer asked.

"My name is Revere," Paul told him.

"What . . . Paul Revere?"

"Yes," Paul answered.

The officers were pleased they'd caught the famous Storm Warning. They happily set off for Lexington with Paul in the middle of them. One of the officers held the reins of Paul's horse so he couldn't get away.

Half a mile from Lexington, they heard a gunshot.

"What was that for?" one officer asked.

"To alarm the country," Paul told him.

Suddenly, the officers were in too much of a hurry to bother with Paul, even if he was the Storm Warning. One officer's horse was very tired. So he got off his horse and took Paul's. The officer cut the saddle and reins off his horse. That way Paul couldn't ride it. Then the officers galloped down the road toward Lexington.

Paul hurried across the fields on foot. He wanted to see what was happening. Had John Hancock and Samuel Adams escaped?

When he got back to the pastor's house, the two men were still arguing. John Hancock had spent all night getting ready to fight. He had

Riding Brown Beauty, one of the fastest horses in Massachusetts, Paul narrowly escapes capture by the British soldiers.

cleaned and prepared his gun and sword.

It was almost dawn before Hancock finally decided Adams was right. Hancock and Adams weren't soldiers. Their minds were far more important to the Patriots than their guns. Finally they left Lexington. Paul and Mr. Lowell, John Hancock's clerk, went with them.

Before they'd gone very far, Paul and Mr. Lowell turned around. Mr. Hancock had left a trunk behind filled with important papers. He didn't want the British to find it.

The church bell was still ringing when Paul and Mr. Lowell reached Lexington. The minutemen's drum was also pounding. Around 50 or 60 minutemen, mostly farmers, were lining up on the common. The common was a meadow-like area in the middle of town. Paul and Lowell hurried into Buckman's Tavern. The large wooden building stood beside the common. That's where the trunk had been left.

Paul looked out the second-story window. British soldiers in their bright red coats and black boots were just reaching town. In the front were the officers who had stopped Paul and taken his horse.

Lowell and Paul found the trunk and carried it down the stairs. They crossed the common just behind the minutemen. Paul heard the captain of the minutemen tell his men not to fire unless the British fired first. Paul and Lowell kept walking as fast as they could.

Bang! They had barely left the common when Paul heard a shot fired. He turned his head to look. He couldn't tell who had fired the first shot. He saw smoke in front of the British troops. A moment later, lots of shots were fired.

Paul and Lowell carried the trunk quickly to the pastor's house. They made it without being shot themselves. They had saved the trunk with its precious papers.

In a few minutes, the fighting was over. Eight minutemen and one British soldier had been killed.

It was April 19, 1775. The Revolutionary War had begun.

The Battle of Bunker Hill was an important early battle fought around Boston at the start of the war. Paul's good friend, Dr. Joseph Warren, fought and was killed there.

6

Grandfather Paul

It was too dangerous for Paul to live in Boston. He wrote a note to his wife, Rachel. He told her to bring the children and meet him outside of Boston. They moved seven miles away to Watertown. Paul's friend, Dr. Joseph Warren, moved to Watertown, too.

Paul Revere made more rides to tell other towns what was happening in Boston and Lexington. But now he had another important job to do for the Patriots. Massachusetts needed money to fight the war. Paul was chosen to make the money.

Dr. Warren was made leader of the Massachusetts

militia. He was in a famous battle near Boston. It was called the Battle of Bunker Hill. Paul was sad when Dr. Warren died in that battle.

Paul kept busy helping the Patriots. He learned how to make gunpowder for the Patriot soldiers. He learned how to make cannons for the soldiers, too. It was with Paul's gunpowder and cannons that many battles were won by the Patriot soldiers.

Paul Revere was not only a skilled silversmith, he was also good at many other things. One of Boston's foremost Sons of Liberty, he printed the first issue of continental currency, made the nation's first official seal, and learned to make gunpowder. He had a total of 16 children—eight with his first wife and eight with his second wife.

A year after the Battle of Lexington, the British soldiers left Boston for good. They were still fighting battles in other places, just not in Boston. So Paul's family moved back to Boston.

Paul was soon made an officer in the Massachusetts militia. He was in charge of the militia at Castle Island–the very place the British had jailed him years before for being a spy. Paul's

A version of an early design from which Paul made the first U.S. seal. The seal was used for all official documents.

son, young Paul, was in the militia then and at the Castle too.

While Paul was at Castle Island he and Rachel had a child. They named the new baby boy Joseph Warren Revere after Paul's very good friend, Dr. Joseph Warren.

Paul and his militia men didn't stay at the Castle all the time. Sometimes, they left and fought nearby battles and then returned.

After the war Paul went back to being a silversmith. He also opened a hardware store. He made church bells, and he made copper for the bottom of ships. Paul even covered Boston's new statehouse dome with copper. Later he started a fire insurance company. One year he was asked to be a health officer for the city of Boston. Paul liked to keep busy and try new things.

Most of Paul and Rachel's children were born during the Revolutionary War. Two of them died young. Paul's children begged him to tell them the story of his ride to Lexington.

Years later his 19 grandchildren also begged him to tell them the story. They thought it was so very exciting!

And so it was.

GLOSSARY

admiral—an officer in the navy or coast guard

ammunition—materials for use in attacks, such as bullets, gunpowder, cannons and cannonballs

apprentice—a person learning a trade from a skilled worker

baptize—to give a baby a Christian name during a church ceremony

battery—a place where ammunition and weapons were kept

common—a piece of land owned by a town, not by any one person

express rider—a person who carried messages by horseback

fife—a wooden flute with finger holes and no keys

hymnbook—a collection of church songs

lobster-backs—nickname for British soldiers because of their bright red coats

Long Room Club—the secret group that led the Sons of Liberty

loyalists—People who believed the American colonies should continue to belong to Great Britain

militia—a group of civilian men called into the military only during emergencies

minutemen—fighting Patriots, called minutemen because they were ready to fight at a minute's notice

patriots–people who believed America should be a country separate from Britain

peninsula–a piece of land with water on three sides

pesthouse–a building where people with sicknesses that spread easily were sent

powder horn–horn of an animal used to carry gunpowder

redcoats–nickname for British soldiers because of their bright red coats

regulars–British soldiers

Sons of Liberty–secret club of Patriots

wharf–a huge dock where ships unload

CHRONOLOGY

1735   Baptized on January 1 in Boston, Massachusetts.

1754   Father dies in July; takes over silversmith duties.

1756   Joins Massachusetts militia; goes to Fort William Henry; duty over in November.

1757   Marries Sara Orne on August 4.

1758   First child, Deborah, born on April 8.

1770   Boston Massacre takes place on March 5.

1773   First wife, Sara, dies; marries Rachel Walker; first ride as express rider on November 30; Boston Tea Party takes place on December 16.

1774   Britain closes Boston Harbor on June 1.

1775   Famous ride to Lexington on April 18; Battle of Lexington takes place on April 19; Battle of Bunker Hill takes place on June 17.

1776   Becomes an officer in the Massachusetts militia.

1813   Second wife, Rachel, dies on June 26.

1818   Dies on May 10.

REVOLUTIONARY WAR TIME LINE ——

1765 The Stamp Act is passed by the British. Violent protests against it break out in the colonies.

1766 Britain ends the Stamp Act.

1767 Britain passes a law that taxes glass, painter's lead, paper, and tea in the colonies.

1770 Five colonists are killed by British soldiers in the Boston Massacre.

1773 People are angry about the taxes on tea. They throw boxes of tea from ships in Boston harbor into the water. It ruins the tea. The event is called the Boston Tea Party.

1774 The British pass laws to punish Boston for the Boston Tea Party. They close Boston harbor. Leaders in the colonies meet to plan a response to these actions.

1775 The battles of Lexington and Concord begin the American Revolution.

1776 The Declaration of Independence is signed. France and Spain give money to help the Americans fight Britain. Nathan Hale is captured by the British. He is charged with being a spy and is executed.

1777 Leaders choose a flag for America. The American troops win some important battles over the British. General Washington and his troops spend a very cold, hungry winter in Valley Forge.

1778 France sends ships to help the Americans win the war. The British are forced to leave Philadelphia.

1779 French ships head back to France. The French support the Americans in other ways.

1780 Americans discover that Benedict Arnold is a traitor. He escapes to the British. Major battles take place in North and South Carolina.

1781 The British surrender at Yorktown.

1783 A peace treaty is signed in France. British troops leave New York.

1787 The U.S. Constitution is written. Delaware becomes the first state in the Union.

1789 George Washington becomes the first president. John Adams is vice president.

FURTHER READING

Barner, Bob. *Which Way to the Revolution? A Book About Maps.* New York: Holiday House, 1998.

Brandt, Keith. *Paul Revere, Son of Liberty.* Mahwah, NJ: Troll Associates, 1982.

Byers, Helen. *Kidding Around Boston: A Young Person's Guide.* Santa Fe, NM: John Muir, 1993.

Forbes, Esther. *America's Paul Revere.* Boston: Houghton Mifflin, 1990.

Ford, Barbara. *Paul Revere: Rider for the Revolution.* Springfield, NJ: Enslow Publishers, 1997.

Fritz, Jean. *And Then What Happened, Paul Revere?* New York: Coward, McCann & Geoghegan, 1973. Reissued by Turtleback, 1996.

Glubok, Shirley. *Home and Child Life in Colonial Days.* New York: Macmillan, 1969.

PICTURE CREDITS

INDEX

ABOUT THE AUTHOR

JOANN A. GROTE loves to read and write about history. She has written over 20 historical novels for adults and children. Her short stories and articles have been published in magazines including *'Teen* and *Guideposts for Kids.* JoAnn worked at the historical restoration of Old Salem in Winston-Salem, North Carolina, for five years. Today she lives in Minnesota.

Senior Consulting Editor **ARTHUR M. SCHLESINGER, JR.** is the leading American historian of our time. He won the Pulitzer Prize for his book *The Age of Jackson* (1945), and again for *A Thousand Days* (1965). This chronicle of the Kennedy Administration also won a National Book Award. He has written many other books, including a multi-volume series, *The Age of Roosevelt.* Professor Schlesinger is the Albert Schweitzer Professor of the Humanities at the City University of New York, and has been involved in several other Chelsea House projects, including the Colonial Leaders series of biographies on the most prominent figures of early American history.